I'm Just Joan

(and I'll Keep on Dancing!)

I'm Just Joan

(and I'll Keep on Dancing!)

by

Joan Martin

with Vicki L. julian

DEDICATION

For my daughter Jonell and granddaughter
Erin; and my son Steve, daughter-in-law
Denise, and grandson Werner.

Joan Hagan

TABLE OF CONTENTS

INTRODUCTION

Blessed! That's how I describe myself. Born in Lawrence, Kansas in 1931 as Joan Hagan, I've been witness to some of the more turbulent times in America, and I've watched both the growth and regression of social interactions among the inhabitants of our melting pot nation. But my story is a little different than what many people would expect.

In my 87 years, I've lived a very good life, met some interesting and famous people along the way, and had some truly exceptional experiences like vacationing on a yacht and flying in a Lear jet. But to explain how all of this happened, I need to start from my humble beginnings and how it influenced me throughout my life.

Joan's parents Sylvester and Ruth

I would not be who I am today except for being blessed with wonderful parents who taught me how to get along with other people; most importantly, they taught me to be comfortable with who I am. Their loving guidance, care and wisdom have seen me through some of the worst and most challenging times, particularly growing up black during the years of racial segregation.

Although I encountered the occasional prejudice, my life has centered on all the things I can do and have done. I prefer to just think of myself as any other human being – not as an African-American woman, not as a divorcee, not as an octogenarian. I'll leave labels up to other people who need them because I only see myself as just Joan.

CHILDHOOD

As the first born child to young parents, the word is that the doctor was late for my delivery and showed up inebriated so my two grandmothers delivered me. I grew up in a very integrated neighborhood. In fact my elementary school, Cordley, was also filled with white and black students, and I played and interacted with my classmates just as I did my neighbors.

My parents told me Cordley divided classes into two categories: one for general education and one focused on college. This was interesting since a decision had to be made regarding a child's future as early as kindergarten. My parents always dreamt of college in my future.

I was fortunate to live nearby both my maternal and paternal grandparents as we all resided within two blocks of each other. Initially, my parents and I actually lived with one set of grandparents until we moved to our house on Tennessee Street. It had an outdoor toilet which my father quickly rectified by building on to our two bedroom abode. It was wonderful to have inside plumbing, and I remember people actually coming over to see what my father built. But I was always envious of one neighbor who had an outdoor facility with two holes!

Our neighborhood was a wonderful place to grow up, and not just because of the central location of our family. We had characters!

One of the most memorable was Miss K at the end of the block. She was a warm and friendly older lady who loved children, and her home was often an afterschool hangout for many of us. Miss K was well thought of in the community, but she had one secret (or so she thought) and his name was Geo.

Geo was a snappy dresser when he went "calling," and we always knew he was headed to Miss K's house when he passed by ours. Although he tried to be discreet, he just wasn't the type to blend into the background. Always a nice man, he would nod and say, "Hello," and sometimes he would even walk his horses down the side street.

I remember my dad always being amused by any of Geo's attempts to be casual in his direction for a stroll. As soon as he was out of hearing, my dad would summon my mother with a chuckle, "Ruth! Ruth! There he goes again!" I didn't know about romantic trysts then so I couldn't quite understand why my dad thought this was so funny.

We also had some difficult people in our community, and I recall how my mother handled one situation with her humor and wit. There was a church nearby that was attended by many in the neighborhood, including a widow who resided close to us. But she was nothing like Miss K! This woman loved to judge others and tell them of their sins. She didn't like the short dresses my mother made for me, or that my mother's arms were uncovered when it was hot, so one day, she admonished my mother. "You're going to Hell," she proclaimed. My mother, who was a godly woman herself but had had enough replied, "Then you'll be the first one I see there, Miss B" After that, the woman kept opinions to herself.

My parents didn't really attend church regularly although they were believers in God and considered themselves Christian. Mostly, I went to church with my grandparents, but Mom would occasionally take me to St. Luke's where her parents attended. It was a

Methodist congregation which I liked because they let me take communion.

Once, when I was four, I was taken to a nearby Baptist church. I went up to the railing and took the sacramental cup as it was passed. The deacon snatched it out of my hands so quickly I almost cried, and it was then I vowed I'd never go back to that church again. My vow was kept and now I'm a Lutheran!

Only once do I recall being an outsider among my grade school classmates. One little girl had a birthday party and I was not invited, but all of the white girls in my Girl Scout troop were. I honestly don't know if it was a racial issue or not. My feelings were hurt, but I always tried to remember what my parents taught me. Sometimes it isn't me or what I am. It's just ignorance on the part of other people. I never let racism alter my feelings for any other nationality – my mother and father taught me well.

My grandparents were also a joy to visit and it was a special treat to ride in my grandfather's car. He worked for the post office, mostly janitorial work, but to me, he was a king. He also cleaned offices and took me with him on occasion. When he let me help empty ash trays, it felt so special because I thought I was doing grown-up work.

He was such an important part of my life and helped instill in me a good work ethic. On the social side, he was also very active in The Shriner's and was later a major influence in my becoming a part of the women's branch of the organization. As a potentate, he held the highest ranking in the organization.

Joan's maternal grandfather Bud Wallace

Although I loved my grandfather dearly, I was definitely a daddy's girl. A boy in my class offered to buy me a bracelet with little charms. I told him not to because, "my Daddy's going to buy me one." I have no idea why I said that except anything I wanted, my father usually bought for me.

When I was 8, I received my first kiss. A boy, whose mother often visited to play cards with my mother, sat on the porch with me. As we were talking, he leaned over and gave me a kiss on the cheek. My response? I gave him a good whack!

I remained enamored with my dad even after my little brother came along when I was 10. Sylvester, Jr. was so cute and I considered myself his second mother.

Holidays and Celebrations

Holidays were always fun in the 40s and 50s. For Halloween, we created our own costumes and then trick-or-treated around the neighborhood. But, as we grew older, there were usually parties at friends' homes where we bobbed for apples and danced. And dancing was one of my favorite things to do!

As I became a little older, I especially liked going to one girl's home for a party because she always served Coca-Cola, tuna sandwiches, and chips. We made costumes from whatever we could conjure up from the closet, and then exacted minor mischief such as putting the fallen leaves on porches and turning over outhouses. Thankfully, we never got caught.

We always had great Christmases too, but some of my earlier gifts were a little unusual, at least by most standards. When I was very young, my parents went to Topeka to try to find a "colored" doll; they knew such a thing did not exist in Lawrence, Kansas. Fortunately, they did find a light-tan porcelain doll with black Shirley Temple curls. She wore a pink dress and I thought she was the most beautiful doll I had ever seen.

Then, when I was around 4 years old, my dad really wanted to buy me an electric train, and I'm not sure that my mom was in total agreement. I remember that it was a yellow and brown Streamliner that had a light and blew smoke. I thought it was so wonderful, but I always had to wait to play with it until my dad and his friends finished playing with it too. When I got older, I realized why dad wanted me to have that train so much – it was really his toy!

My parents convinced me and my little brother we had a Santa's helper named Pete living in our attic, and he reported on our behavior directly to Santa Claus. We believed this so strongly that we tried to get on Pete's good side by baking him cookies. Fortunately, Pete must have always had good things to say because we received the gifts we wanted.

But on one occasion, when my little brother was 3 months old, all I wanted for Christmas was a pair of white boots. My parents told me they could not afford to get those for me and I was crushed. When we opened gifts on Christmas morning, my mom told me to open the gift for my little brother which I thought was a baby blanket. It turned out those were the boots I desperately wanted, and I felt so grown-up and snazzy!

My parents also had a good time surprising each other with their gifts. One Christmas, my dad included me in his little conspiracy when he bought my mom a beautiful new negligée which he knew she would love. He wrapped it and put it under their bed. After all the gifts were opened Christmas morning, he told me to go retrieve it. When Mom opened the box, she was more than disappointed − it was her old holey nightgown! I had to stifle a laugh because I knew what was to come. When my dad quit smiling, he told her to look underneath the well-worn garment, and there was the beautiful replacement negligée.

While I can remember many wonderful Christmases, I recall the one year that my dad was in the doghouse for bringing home what my mother thought was an unacceptable tree. Someone had given him the tree and he insisted, even with its exaggerated leaning, "there's nothing wrong with that tree."

Dad was mostly right. With enough decorations, our "Charlie Brown tree" turned out to be acceptable, but dad never brought home a less than perfect tree again.

My most vivid memory of Easter, besides hunting for eggs and receiving Easter baskets and nests with candy, was when my grandmother wanted to buy me a fancy dress for the holiday. We made a special trip to a nice department store and the clerk immediately tried to direct us to the sales rack. My grandmother kept her composure, but ignored the sales clerk and instead went to the pretty little dresses on the display rack for Easter. After we picked out two dresses for purchase, my grandmother made a point of talking with the clerk in private. I know it probably wasn't a nice conversation, but I was more interested in my pretty new Easter dresses.

ADOLESCENCE

Puberty came early for me, but I played with paper dolls until I was 16. These weren't just child's play; the Sunday paper had celebrity figures that could be cut out along with several outfits. I felt like a fashion designer dressing the likes of Deanna Durbin, Errol Flynn, Shirley Temple, Van Johnson, Dorothy Lamour, John Wayne, and others. They were always printed in color, and I guess it gave me a sense of knowing I could interact with the elite, which of course, I later did. My dad liked movie stars too, especially Joan Crawford after whom I was named. He was crazy about her!

Later, when I started going to the movies regularly, I cut pictures from magazines about the shows and posted them all over my bedroom walls. Westerns and love stories were my favorites. I could always identify with the stories that had a princess in them because that's how I felt – like royalty in my family. And when my parents arranged dancing and piano lessons, I felt like a very talented princess!

When I reached junior high school, my parents allowed me to go downtown by myself. I liked to visit my cousin Maxine who was one of the first black girls to work behind the counters at the Kresge Department store as a sales clerk. She became employed after a march on Massachusetts Street to promote hiring more black girls to work in the stores. She was not allowed to handle monetary transactions, only to help the customers with selecting their purchases.

In junior high, we had classes in different buildings depending upon the subject. High school was called Liberty Memorial and is now the location for Central Middle School.

At this same time in the 1940s, blacks were only allowed to order at the counter of many cafes and stores with food service. There was no place for us to eat what we bought, except outside − booths and tables were reserved for white people only. I never thought too much about it because that was just the way things were, however; I can honestly say I've never been anywhere when I personally felt out of place or that I didn't belong. But, there was one uncomfortable situation which I describe in the next chapter.

Recognition of my artistic talent also took place around this same time. In high school, art students were given the opportunity to paint a mural for Christmas. This was fun for me because I already had experience doing murals as backdrops for the Delta and Alpha black sororities at KU for their fashion shows. I even modeled in some of them while in junior high and high school. My connection with the sororities actually even preceded the murals – when I was 8, I danced in one of their fashion shows.

In high school, we had two basketball teams – one for whites and one for blacks. There was a separate pep club (of which I was a member) for the black team known as "The Promoters." We never got to travel to any of their games like the white pep club, and we didn't wear anything to distinguish ourselves as an organized group.

One day, four of us finally decided to go to the principal, Mr. Wherry, and ask why we couldn't have special uniforms like the white team's pep club. He readily agreed and ordered special jackets just for us. To augment the uniform, we wore pleated skirts and

black and white oxford shoes. And did
we look classy!

INTEGRATION

Integration happened, but sometimes just not publicly. Most in the black community knew of white businessmen (some pillars of the community and even married) who courted black women, but it was never discussed openly.

When I was in junior high, I spent time with three friends who were all artistic and white. On one particular occasion, we were working on a mural for the school and decided to walk a few blocks to eat downtown.

As we sat down in the booth of a local drug store, the waitress came over and said, "Our manager said I can serve you (talking to my friends and then looking at me), but I can't serve her." I was dumbfounded and hurt, but my friends retaliated with their own act of defiance. "If you can't serve her, then we're all leaving." At that, all four of us calmly walked out of the store.

It hurt rather than angered me that I was refused service. But even though I told my friends, "You girls stay and eat, and I'll go outside," it made me feel good that my friends stood up for me. I knew other places where blacks could only order from the counter, but I didn't realize this was one that wouldn't even allow me to buy food. Still, I never felt like a second class citizen. My self-esteem, thanks to my parents, was never affected and I never felt inferior.

I can't remember anyone ever calling me the "N" word. I've never thought much about the word itself, but I still don't understand why it's so offensive to some blacks who think nothing of it to call each other. In fact, I think the word has always been a little funny to me.

Before I was 16, my father cleaned out the garage for someone who had an old Victrola. He was given the old record player along with some records which found their way to my room. By then, hi-fis were the thing so no one minded my propriety.

There was one old record my cousin James and I played over and over. I don't recall the name of the song, but the most memorable lyrics were: "Bake that pie, Nigger-Nigger." We played that line over and over until the record slowed to a stop, laughing all the while. Sometimes, we even slowed the record down to elongate the words we found to be so hilarious. And although many people are offended by the use of the word to mean lazy and no good, I think it wasn't bothersome because I never felt those descriptions applied to me. I still laugh every time I think of that record, and I wish I had a copy.

It was funny, too, that sometimes segregation worked against those who enforced it. In particular, black people had to sit in the balcony of local theatres. It turned out this was actually the best place to view the movies! It just so happened that one of my very first dates was to the theater, and I loved viewing the show from the best seats.

I dated frequently until I married. My first boyfriend was a high school athlete, and I remained friends with him until he passed away in 2018. At one time, I even dated 3 boys who all went by the name of Sonny. It was great – I never worried about calling them by the wrong name, but it was terribly confusing when I talked about any of them!

While in high school, I also met my future husband, who was attending KU, when my cousin James brought him over for a visit. Mason lived at home while attending college and he was such a gentleman! I even bragged to my friends that he respected me so much, I never had to worry about him trying to take advantage like most teenage boys my age.

At that time, there were no on-campus dorms for black men and women. Even black fraternity and sorority members had to live off campus in the homes of other colored families who hosted them. Because of their close proximity to campus, at one time, both sets of my grandparents opened their homes to students – one, a girl; the other, a boy.

Mason was two years older than I, but I did my best to project a mature attitude. After all, I was a high schooler and he was a college man.

Once, I slipped out at night to meet him and go dancing. I thought my little ruse was successful until I realized, upon returning home, a shoe was missing. My parents asked me about it, but I feigned innocence about where it could be.

Maybe my parents had suspicions and realized they were just better off not knowing the details, but the matter soon dropped. I still continued to go dancing because I loved it, but I made sure not to lose any more shoes.

Although I thought I would attend KU, my aunt in Chicago arranged for me to be accepted and attend the Chicago Institute of Art after graduation. I was visiting her that summer when Mason asked me to come home before I enrolled because he had something for me. It turned out to be an engagement ring. By then, I had fallen in love, so my plans to attend college and study fine arts fell through when Mason asked me to marry him. I don't regret my decision as I have two wonderful children from that marriage, and art has always remained an important part of my life.

FIRST ENCOUNTER WITH A DIFFERENT SIDE OF LIFE

Soon after marriage, I began working for Dick Williams as his cook. Those familiar with the Williams Foundation at KU will recognize this esteemed family member. He was a kind and gentle man who led an interesting social and personal life.

I began working for Mr. Williams, mostly doing housekeeping chores, when my cousin Delores needed an assistant. She was working as the cook and recommended me. I had a very quick interview with only three questions, but the one I remember was, "Do you drink a lot?!"

Delores and her husband Rudolph both began working for Mr. Williams when they moved back to Lawrence after Rudolph's studies at Kansas State were finished. While in Manhattan, she and Rudolph lived with the Milton Eisenhower family doing much of the same as they did later for Mr. Williams – Delores cooked and Rudolph helped to serve at dinner.

Their time in Lawrence was equally enjoyed while Rudolph was studying at KU to become a doctor. Delores became pregnant just as they prepared to move to St. Louis for his internship. Giving notice, she told Mr. Williams of her joyous news. He thought a great deal of her and didn't want her to leave, but replied, "Well, whose fault was that?" and laughed and laughed. We all got a chuckle out of his little banter.

After Delores left, I became the cook, and my new husband became the one to bartend at parties and serve at dinner. We did this while Mason was going to KU.

Even with new employment, we still had time for our own fun social activities, especially attending parties where dancing was a main attraction. It was fun to be among others such as Wilt Chamberlain. Wilt was always a guest at parties during his year at KU in 1957-58, and Mason received plenty of invitations, even after leaving KU.

When Mason finally decided he wanted to do something else and not finish his college education, he chose to work for the post office in Kansas City. Initially, he commuted, and I still remained at the Williams' home since apartments in K.C. were very limited. We had to be placed on a waiting list, but that meant I needed a car to have in Lawrence while Mason was at work in another city.

When I mentioned this to Mr. Williams, he said, "Go find one and we'll have it looked over." I chose a '49 white Buick, which he paid for, and let payments come out of my paycheck. I'm not entirely sure I paid off my debt because he said I didn't have to.

Working for this gentleman was a delight, and he trusted me implicitly, just like Delores. He had an account at the grocery store at 19th and Mississippi and it was my duty to buy groceries every week to supplement the deliveries of meat and Coca-Cola to the home. Meat went into one of four freezers, and the spirit deliveries for parties were handled by Mason who took it to the attic. Of course, I had keys to the attic too!

Mr. Williams was never concerned with what or how much I bought, even while he was in Europe and I continued to take care of his home. Now I understood why he asked me in the interview if I drank a lot. He wanted someone he could trust to watch over the booze!

Of course, the refrigerator was always stocked with game since Mr. Williams was a hunter. We also had plenty of adult beverages, a perk of his liquor store ownership. At dinner, there were always two plates for serving – one for meat and one for vegetables, and there was the stereotypical buzzer under the table to summon Mason if needed.

Anything I wanted, Mr. Williams was sure to provide. Although I had an account set up at Weaver's Department Store, which he paid for, all I had to do was ask for anything if they didn't offer it.

Once I ordered all new carpet for the living room, dining room and hall. When I became concerned about security and ordered all new screens for the windows in the back of the house, I was a little worried that he might not think the expense was justified. I needn't have worried because he walked me to the porch and laughed saying, "I just love it. It's wonderful!"

I also visited his office once a week to clean and tidy it up a bit. There, he also kept a storeroom full of toasters and other items which he offered to clients and friends. Whenever there was a wedding or birthday of a business associate, he told me to go pick out something they might like. I always had a key so it was no problem.

Mr. Williams worked as a bookkeeper for Miss Watkins, for whom the city's historical museum and hospital on the KU campus in Lawrence, Kansas are named. He was already divorced when I was employed and had an active social life as a member of a gun club as well as many other social groups. He often hosted friends from Texas who came on a chartered bus on Saturday morning to attend the KU football game. They partied all night, and suffice it to say, they were all members of the elite and wealthy class. They left on Sunday and there was always much to do to get the house back in order for which I always received extra pay.

My standard fare to serve the group was chili, one of Mr. Williams' favorite dishes. He could dine on any cuisine he wished, but his tastes were often simple. That was my first realization that people are people, even those who are more affluent.

I was once invited to a chili cook-off in Texas by one of his guests. Mr. Williams took me aside and said, "Look, you're a grown woman, but I'll be in Europe and can't protect you against any unsolicited advances. I wish you wouldn't go." Even though I might have won the contest, I opted not to go since Mr. Williams didn't want me to.

I loved being privy to the Williams' social life, both father and son. During this time, Mr. Williams' son Odd was also going to KU and living at home. He had much the same personality as his father so it was always nice to care for him when his father was away. Since Mr. Williams owned 12 farms in Western Kansas and traveled a lot, even abroad, I often found myself just ensuring that the household remained intact.

Odd had a girlfriend named Jonell, whom he later married, and I truly adored her. She was so sweet and belonged to one of the sororities at KU. In fact, I liked her so much that I later named my daughter after her.

As soon as an apartment became available in Kansas City, I left Mr. Williams' employment. After we moved there to be where Mason worked for the post office, I later also wanted a job. Jonell was just a baby so I thought I could find someone to watch her.

Although jobs were scarce for black girls, I began looking at the want ads. I found one at a prominent department store downtown looking for a girl to run the elevator, but my hopes were dashed when it said "looking for a light-skinned colored girl." This is the one time I actually remember being angry about discrimination.

Soon after, I was expecting our second child, Stevie, when I got a job window dressing in a small boutique that catered to the wealthy. It was interesting when some of the women came in the store to buy a dress for a special occasion, and then asked to take at least two home to show their husbands for their opinion of which one to purchase. A few days later, they would return and say neither dress suited their husbands, and since the tags were still attached, the boutique graciously accepted the return. The interesting part is that we all knew at least one dress had been worn.

After the women left, we just shook our heads and laughed at the idea of these women thinking they got away with something. It was proof that even some rich people, who could afford such clothing, were not above taking advantage.

During our time in K.C., Mason built our home with a loan from the Veterans Administration. It was in a very nice area of Kansas City called Sheraton Estates.

Just down the road from us lived the relative of Jazz legend Jay McShann. My daughter became friends with the McShann girl while they attended school and scouts, and then Pete McShann's wife Jessie and I became good friends. I was delighted to discover they were related to the jazz great, and when Jay came to KC, we were invited to their home.

After the club where Jay was playing closed, he brought his band to Pete's home where the two brothers jammed – Pete on drums and Jay on piano. I sometimes sang the blues along with them, and we partied into the wee hours of the morning while our children slept.

MISCELLANEOUS EMPLOYMENT

After divorcing Mason, when my son was in early grade school and my daughter was in junior high, we moved to a rented home on 32nd Street in Kansas City. By then, I was working at St. Luke's Hospital.

As a new member of the nursing support staff, one of my first tasks was to administer an enema to one of the patients. It was what we called the 3 Hs for high, hot and a helluvalot! I requested the gentleman assume a particular position, and tried to be as gracious as I could. I had no idea he was one of the top administrators for the hospital. Later, I was called into the nursing supervisor's office and was scared out of my mind for fear I'd done something wrong. Instead, she informed me of the patient's importance and what he said – I was one of the most professional staff members he had seen. After that, I was always assigned male patients!

I later became an OB technician. Initially everything was fine, but by the time my children were teenagers, it was a volatile period in the history of our country. Racial conflict had turned bloody, and although I never had concerns for myself, I worried about my children.

I reared my son and daughter in the same way my parents reared me – there were no "victims" in my family. People were people, and those who didn't understand that were just ignorant – exactly the same sentiments I learned as a child from my parents. My father always said, "If someone treats you differently because of your color, ignore them. They just don't know any better." It was his advice I took in realizing my place in the world. That's what I wanted for my kids too.

Perhaps the scariest moment for me was while we were living in this same location which was near the plaza, and I was working at St. Luke's as an Obstetrics Technician. When race relations became strained, there was concern about the stores on the Plaza and no one was allowed into the area without reason. I was given a pass for work to enter the Plaza area just to travel to and from the hospital.

We were watching TV one night after feasting on chipped beef on toast (you always remember the silliest things in stressful moments) when gunshots rang out nearby. I quickly made sure the windows were covered, and locked the doors when the lights suddenly went out. I crawled to the window to see gunfire, and focused on our safety. I rapidly moved myself and my children to the bathroom, with a large quilt in tow, where we spent the night on the floor praying. I wasn't about to peek outside again to watch the commotion, and to this day, I don't know who fired the gun that killed one man on my lawn, if it was a black/white altercation, or if the gunfire was even racially motivated. I just knew this wasn't how I wanted to live, or what I wanted for my children.

Things did calm down after that night and I remained in the same location. I felt safe because the building was six units and we were on the bottom floor across the hall from the building's owners. After Jonell was in high school and Steve in Jr. High, we moved to Van Brunt Street.

While all of the conflict was occurring, I loved my position at St. Luke's – assisting doctors, sterilizing and dispensing equipment, and preparing expectant mothers to give birth. Later, on several occasions, when the doctor was delayed or the baby came sooner than expected, I delivered the babies!

I remember my first solo delivery. Strangely enough, it wasn't that big of an issue for me. I'd been part of the team that delivered hundreds of babies, and I felt confident in handling the delivery as long as it was a normal one.

On this particular occasion, the doctor was still trying to scrub in and change clothes while a team of us were already in the delivery room with the mother. The baby couldn't wait so I handled the delivery while the doctor stood peering through the doors overseeing the event with a smile. He did finally enter to finish the post-delivery activities, much to my relief. After a while, no one worried if the doctor was delayed because they knew I could handle it. And I did…for 13 years.

It was an amazing experience at St. Luke's, and I was even encouraged to take classes to further my medical education. I loved the doctors and my co-workers, and became close friends with one of the obstetricians. He often invited me and my children to his home so that Jonell and Steve could swim with his children. Our close friendship made me aware of many of his kindnesses which he chose to keep secret.

Later, when I was living in California and my daughter was still in Kansas City, she gave birth to my granddaughter at St. Luke's. This same doctor was in the delivery room, phone in hand, to make me a part of this most precious moment. And that, I never forgot.

It was also during my time at St. Luke's when I had my first art show at Blue Ridge Mall in Kansas City, MO.

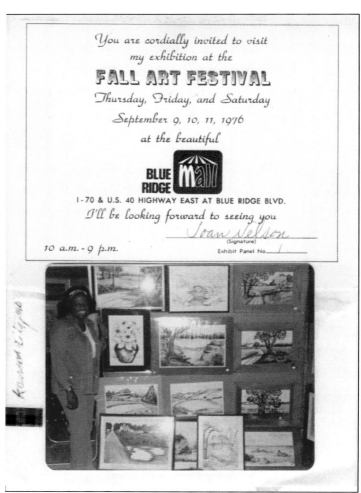

Advertisement for Joan's first art show

A LIFE CHANGING MOVE TO CALIFORNIA

My mother and father separated, but still remained married. My mother, who did not want to divorce, decided to move to California where one of her friends was living. She went into nursing and achieved the equivalent of an LPN certification, and then worked in a hospital in Los Angeles.

While attending school, one of her friends was working for Ricky Nelson, son of Ozzie and Harriet. Her friend needed a substitute, for just one weekend, who could care for Ricky's young family and asked my mother if she were interested. This then became an occasional job for my mother and she enjoyed taking the baby to Ozzie and Harriet's home, attending parties there, and meeting numerous celebrities. She often sent autographed photos of the Nelson family to us, and Jonell cried when the other children would not believe her grandmother worked for them. I simply told her it didn't matter what the other children believed because we knew what was true.

Later, when my children were both in college, I decided to move to California to be near to my mother. California held many surprises and opportunities for me, including my second marriage to Al Martin whom I divorced after just four years. He did take me to Hawaii where we visited a gallery with artwork by Anthony Quinn and Red Skeleton. I spoke with the manager of the gallery, and after learning I was also an artist, he asked for my card. Two months later, I received a call inviting me to an Anthony Quinn art show at the famous

Beverly Hills Wilshire Hotel. When the gallery manager asked if I could attend, I was flabbergasted! Did he expect me to say, "No, I think I'm washing my hair that day?" Of course, I would go!

It turned out to be an elegant affair with Champaign and petite sandwiches, and Anthony Quinn's work was outstanding. It included sculpture, watercolor, oils and acrylics, but mostly sculpture and oils.

Surrounded by all the opulence, and being among this elite crowd, I thought the little black girl from Kansas, who stood on the sidewalk waving at all the passersby, could never have imagined being here. In fact, it was difficult for me to believe I was actually here as I stood in awe of the reality of it all. I kept thinking, *How am I here? I'm just Joan*.

Also during this time, my cousin Barbara's daughter, Cheryl, was married to actor Ted Lange from the TV series

The Love Boat, and they had two beautiful children. Ted was a wonderful person, and my first close relationship with a celebrity. He and Cheryl had many parties at their home which gave me the opportunity to meet many radio and TV stars.

Prior to returning to my preferred profession in hospitals, I had a few odd jobs. One was working in the L.A. Parks and Recreation Department. There, I was supervised by Goldie Hawn's sister, and she taught me to type. I even met Goldie once while we were walking into the studio where she was taping the *Rowan & Martin Laugh In* comedy show. Goldie's sister had given me tickets to be in the audience, and it was such a delight to unexpectedly meet one of the stars. Surprisingly, I didn't think they looked much like sisters.

I first interviewed for a job at Brotsman Hospital but did not get the position I wanted. I loved being an OB tech, but they required it to be filled by a registered nurse. Instead, the human resources representative offered me a job in central supply. Later, this experience served me well when I moved to Westside Hospital and became the unit's assistant manager, and then manager of central supply. This is also the time I acquired my first agent who helped me obtain some of my more interesting positions outside of the art world.

But before I was employed at Westside, I began attending a nearby church. There, I met my second husband who was an usher. Although he was older than I, we began dating, and I then became employed at Westside Hospital.

We had been dating a while when I was accosted in the parking lot by two men who wanted my purse. Fortunately, it was the color of the leather seats in my car and stashed between them so the would-be robbers believed me when I said I didn't have a pocketbook. Afterwards, my soon-to-be husband suggested we get married, and I thought it would be nice to be protected by having him around. Unfortunately, he was a bit more protective than I wanted. I knew he was trying to control me when I came home from work to find he had laid out what I should wear for Valentine's Day, including dress, shoes and jewelry. After four years, we parted company.

Our union actually had a positive effect on my career as an artist. It was Al who first suggested framing one of my paintings. When the framer told me, "Young lady, this painting is going to do something for you. It's very good," I didn't realize how right he was about my future. It was the first painting I actually sold, and that was later to my daughter-in-law's sister. Strangely enough, I can't recall for how much I sold it, but I do remember its title – "Sweet Pear."

Sweet Pear (with Blue Ribbon)

This all came about when that painting was entered into a juried art show at an art museum on Wilshire Blvd. I was thrilled to have my work accepted because there were three floors of fantastic paintings that I thought were fabulous…about 500 entries into the contest.

Three days after entering my artwork, a woman from the museum asked if I planned to attend the reception at the art show. "Of course!" I replied.

I arrived and sat at one of the tables while they gave out awards in various categories. I was talking when the final category, which happened to be watercolor, was announced. When the emcee said, "Would Joan Martin please come to the stage?" my legs suddenly became weak and I almost fainted! It still seems surreal to me.

Westside Hospital also afforded me one of the most exciting moments of my medical career when I was awarded "Employee of the Year." There were two parties: one at the Marina, and one at a large Beverly Hills hotel. That came with the bonus of a large check from the doctors, and I have the photo of me descending the staircase in the hotel where I received my award as well as the plaque they gave to me.

Award ceremony for Employee of the Year (now hanging on Joan's wall)

While in L.A., I later had an art show in a large bank. I guess someone really liked my work because they stole one of three themed paintings. That was the only time I've ever had a painting stolen and I don't know whether to be more upset or honored that they liked my painting enough to steal it!

During this time, I also maintained my membership in the Shriner's, as did Al, and I even managed to help publish two cookbooks, one for the Church of

Religious Science in Claremont where I later taught art classes, and the other devoted to my recipes and those of my mother and aunts. I even took art classes myself for two years at West Los Angeles College.

Working at Westside afforded me many opportunities with my art. They wanted to stage an art show and asked me to organize it. There, I displayed my artwork as well as other artists, and it became a tremendous success. After that, I did three art shows with L.A. Parks and Recreation and met Gladys Knight of Gladys Knight and the Pips fame. We had an interesting lunch together while her daughter was having surgery although I can't recall a thing we talked about! I just remember how down to earth she was, and how much I enjoyed meeting her.

While working there, I also met Dick Van Dyke who attended one of my art shows along the coast of Malibu. He spent time looking intently at some of my paintings, but I never knew if he actually purchased one.

In addition to those celebrities, I met singer Nancy Wilson and had drinks with Lou Rawls after friends took me to a fancy establishment where we caught up with him.

I also met Blues great Joe Williams on a cruise where he performed for the "As You Seas" cruise entertainment. I met his wife, too, and we all became fast friends during the voyage. In fact, I still have a ring from Mexico that I bought while shopping with them at one of the ports of call during the cruise.

With Joe was Red Holloway as part of the entertainment aboard ship. My mom spent time with him too as she accompanied me on the cruise along with a white man I was dating.

After moving to Palm Springs to begin a new life, I worked at what I call "Frank

Sinatra's hospital" (he was part owner, I believe). It was also known as the Desert Hospital, and I encountered a number of celebrities, including the famous Gabor sisters who were actresses.

While Eva and Zsa Zsa's mother was a patient, the designer Mr. Blackwell (famous for his "Ten Worst Dressed List"), arrived for a visit. I accompanied him on a tour of the facility, but was surprised he wore an old sweater and dressed somewhat shabbily. I wondered why a fashion expert would even wear something like that!

One of the most interesting people I cared for was Larry Flynt, owner and publisher of the bawdy *Pent House* magazine. I knew of him, but didn't really think anything about serving as one of his nurses. He was never as happy with the care from other nursing assistants, but he took a liking to me and requested that I be his primary nurse. He was also one of the few patients who felt the need to always have a guard outside his door.

MORE OPPORTUNITIES TO LIVE WITH THE "OTHER HALF"

It's always strange to think of the phrase how the "other half lives." That implies that half the people are extremely wealthy when, in fact, half aren't. Only a small fraction can be said to be so, and my next employer definitely was.

After divorcing Al, I acquired an agent for my paintings, and even had some of my work displayed in a gallery. One day the agent called, but it wasn't related to my paintings – a wealthy couple was in need of a cook. Since I had been unemployed a couple of months, I was eager to accept most anything. Because of the connections the position might afford me, I decided to pursue whatever was available.

The agent told me that a cook's position was available in the home of Paul and Lucy Whittier, well known philanthropists and a most delightful couple. Mr. Whittier inherited a number of oil wells in California, owned by his late father, so he was considered "old money." In fact, the home where he was born was featured as a mansion on the "Lives of the Rich and Famous" TV show. Later, it was sold to an Arab of Muslim faith from the Middle East who painted clothes on the statues.

Lucy was Mr. Whittier's second wife and both he and she had adult children from their first marriages – all very nice individuals. I especially came to know the son of Mr. Whittier quite well as they often docked their yachts in the same locations.

Of course, I didn't know anything about the Whittiers at the time the job was mentioned. I was actually just sitting in the agent's office later when Mrs. Whittier called and asked me to come to their home for an interview.

After I interviewed with the couple at their sprawling and elegant home, I was given a tour of the kitchen. It surprised me when a job offer was then given – they didn't even check my references! They were such an engaging elderly couple in their 80s, and the kitchen was a super gourmet facility with all the newest in appliances and gadgets, I had no problem immediately accepting their offer.

While I was touring, another call came from my agent about a woman who was mute, but needed someone to accompany her in her travels for 2 or 3 months. The location would have allowed me to paint while I served as her cook, but I liked the Whittiers, especially when they asked if I could travel with them. Since I'm always eager to go places and try new things, it was an easy decision. They even paid $500 to move my things to their home.

My accommodations were splendid – a suite with all of the expensive accouterments one might expect. There was a separate dressing room from my bedroom, private bath, and living area with elegantly upholstered seating and crystal accent pieces throughout.

On my first day as their new employee, I wanted to do something special for them in appreciation of their hiring me by baking one of my special apple pies. As I began to prepare everything, I pulled out one of the kitchen cabinet drawers and a very heavy slide-out board fell on my foot. They called their doctor in San Diego to make an appointment for me to see him the next day, and then insisted on staying with me the entire day. Mrs. Whittier constantly made offers to help me until Mr. Whittier finally said, "She doesn't need offers of help. What she needs is a drink!"

I was very embarrassed about the accident and sure that my employment would end as quickly as it began. But it didn't, and that was the beginning of when I realized exactly how fortunate it was to work for these wonderful people.

Before I was hired, they had planned to go to their vacation home in Friday Harbor which was actually the day after my accident, and they worried whether I would be well enough to go with them. But they didn't realize I wasn't about to pass up flying on their Lear jet that had two pilots. No matter what the doctor said, I was going!

The Whittier's Lear jet

On the way to Canada, Mr. Whittier made us gimlets while I played Rummy with Mrs. Whittier. The damage to my foot was severe enough to curtail my activities, but it did not stop me from enjoying the first of many trips with my new employers. So, instead of preparing meals for the Whittiers, they took care of me!

It wasn't long before I was considered a part of their family. Mr. Whittier often brought their guests to the kitchen to meet me! I accompanied them on many trips to various locales, including numerous trips to Friday Harbor. We flew on their Lear jet and sailed on their yacht named Paul Lu, a combination of both of their first names – Paul and Lucy.

The Paul Lu

Typically, the Whittiers invited guests on their yacht cruises, and I worked several days in advance preparing meals that needed only to be heated once on board. They had two

70

refrigerators and three freezers, and a shelf that heated the dishes. My duty was to first feed the crew of four, and then the Whittiers and their guests. I ate afterwards with the other woman who accompanied us as the housekeeper on board.

Joan's cabin aboard the yacht

Although I enjoyed the adventures as much as anyone, I often found an extra $500 or so, placed where I could find it, as a special thank you for catering the affair for the Whittier's guests. In the

70s, that was a significant amount of money, and the bonus was simply an expression of their gratitude in addition to my regular salary. I was just happy to tag along to enjoy what I would never have been able to do on my own.

As mentioned earlier, Friday Harbor, near the Canadian border, was a favorite destination of the couple, and we generally spent time at their home there for two months. Of course, they also owned a vacation home in Victoria, Canada, either of which any of us would have been ecstatic to own as our primary residence.

The home in Friday Harbor was nestled in secluded woods and a great place to enjoy nature with walking and bike trails. There, I also had a private suite and was given many opportunities to freely explore the surrounding area, often with extra cash to spend courtesy of the Whittiers. In fact, Mr. Whittier often suggested I just go there to rest up with my family or friends after I catered his business meetings in Seattle.

Golf carts were the mode of transportation on the grounds of our Safety Harbor community

I was even sometimes given the key to the home while taking my own vacation. I could invite family or friends to accompany me, drive the car that remained there for use when the Whittiers visited, and had free reign over the use of their tennis courts and all other amenities on the grounds. And I did avail myself of those many times when hosting my girl friends and family members.

Accommodations at Friday Harbor

On one memorable occasion, it was my birthday and some girlfriends accompanied me. We had high tea, and I'll never forget how very special that felt – a perfect thing to do in Victoria, Canada!

74

Mr. Whittier was well known in the area. Through donations, he helped to build the local hospital, theatre, and several other notable landmarks. It seemed his philanthropy and caring knew no bounds, and he was respected as a member of the community, albeit a vacationing one! He was well known as a supporter of the Scripps Memorial Hospitals in California, establishing the Mericos Eye Institute and The Whittier Institute for Diabetes and Endocrinology within two of their hospitals. He also supported a number of organizations in San Diego such as the San Diego Maritime Museum to which he donated a restored steam ship costing $2 million dollars.

For 16 months, I enjoyed the same comforts and benefits given to the very rich. But the Whittiers also advanced my career as an artist. When one of their guests learned I was an artist, she and Mrs. Whittier asked to see my paintings.

Mrs. Whittier was so excited about finding one she loved, and went promptly back to drag her husband to see all of my artwork. He agreed on her choice and paid me $1000! That was my first big sale. Later, Mr. Whittier facilitated the sale of another of my paintings for $500. He was very encouraging and supportive of my efforts as an artist after exclaiming, "I didn't know you were a painter!" I thought his wife surely must have known because my agent referred me to them.

In addition to helping gain exposure of my artwork, Mr. Whittier began the process of renovating a studio in the Friday Harbor home so that I could paint. He even arranged to have a special showing of my work at the home of Burl Ives. Unfortunately, Mr. Ives passed away before that happened.

After little more than a year with the Whittiers, Mr. Whittier became ill and preferred the services of a male nurse. I was visiting friends in Las Vegas when I received the news he was going into the hospital in San Diego and not expected to return home. Mrs. Whittier packed all of my belongings and sent them to me in Vegas.

I lived with my daughter Jonell, who had since moved to California, while I weighed my options of what to do next. My mother's health also worsened and she passed away during this time. It wasn't long before a few of my girlfriends encouraged me to visit them again in Las Vegas, and I decided to stay.

Circa 1992, I acquired my first job there by looking at the want ads in the paper. That resulted in my employment as a cook with another family. They were a couple without children who kept constantly busy running their specialty stores in Los Angeles, San Diego, Palm Springs and Las Vegas.

Continuously on the lookout for valuable collectibles for their inventory, they were often away while I remained at their home and also served as housekeeper. These wonderful people treated me like family, just as the Whittiers had done.

While in Vegas, I taught art classes with students that included ministers, doctors, and lawyers!

Watercolor Artist

Joan

Lessons • Workshops • Commissions
(702) 362-7161

Joan's first business card

The city also afforded me a wonderful opportunity. Of special note is that this was during the time of the 1985 "We Are the World Movement" – an extraordinary fundraiser to help alleviate famine in

Africa which had reached critical numbers. This effort brought some of the biggest names in music together such as Michael Jackson and Lionel Richey (coauthors of the hit single of the same name as the movement); Harry Belafonte, Ray Charles, Billy Joel, Bruce Springsteen, Diana Ross, Cyndi Lauper, Smokey Robinson, and 5 of Michael Jackson's siblings. I was honored to do some sketches of a few of the artists for a pamphlet advertising the event in Vegas.

Suffice it to say, I was given great support for my artwork, and my new employers became big benefactors in purchasing numerous paintings from me. In fact, the lady of the house's kitchen remains completely decorated with my watercolors.

The kitchen of Joan's Las Vegas employers

I also became acquainted with the woman's parents, and was often a guest at their country club for parties and club events. But the most amazing thing of all to me was really my relationship with everyone. It was so close that Amy* even began calling me her surrogate mother, and it proved once again what my parents always taught me – people are just people.

*Not her real name

I remained with the family for almost fourteen years, until my son Steve wanted me to move back to Lawrence to be near him, and I was happy to do so. So, Midwest, here I came!

Joan's going away party given by her Las Vegas art students

MY LIFE TODAY

My "family ties" established with the last family are so strong that we remain good friends to this day. In fact, I spend time with them whenever I visit the area, and sometimes I just plan a special visit to stay with them so we can go shopping and partake in some of the local entertainment.

My life is no longer surrounded with the luxuries of wealth, but I am rich. I have wonderful children and grandchildren who provide for me when needed, and brighten my day with shared events and memories. I am active in my singles group at church, blessed with many friends, and I still love to cook and share my culinary delights. And, of course, I also dance whenever the opportunity occurs.

At 87, I have slowed down a little, and certainly there are things I have forgotten over almost nine decades. There are also some memories I've chosen not to include in my memoir to protect the innocent (as well as the guilty!). Nevertheless, I still drive and take a bus to the casinos in neighboring cities, and I've just recently stopped teaching my watercolor craft to others. But whenever anyone suggests attendance at a concert or play, I'm one of the first to RSVP.

Adventures in Painting

Explore the basics of painting with local artist and instructor Joan Martin.

Adventures in Painting
Wednesdays, October 11 - November 15
9:00 - 11:00 AM
Prairie Ridge Art Studio
1000 Wakarusa, Lawrence

Six Week Course $75.00
Basic supply list required for this couse.

REGISTER TODAY at www.YourSRC.org
or call 785-842-0543.

Senior Resource Center
for Douglas County

A flyer advertising one of Joan's art classes in Lawrence, KS (courtesy of Douglas County Senior Resources)

Without question, God has been good and allowed me to live a very blessed life. He gave me the best parents, art talent, ability to see the world with wonder and excitement, and the will to make the most of opportunities. In fact, I never say I've lived a good life, I say I'm **having** a good life because I still am! But with all the things I've seen and done, the best thing is being comfortable with who I am...I'm just Joan (and I'm still dancing whenever I can).

Love,

Joan

Joan's one and only poem:

The Rose

The petals so fair

The fragrance so sweet

The colors so soft

Like a lady it unfolds

With charm and grace

A SAMPLE OF JOAN'S PAINTINGS:

Sunflowers (also on the cover)

The Golden Bloom (also on the back cover)

Malibu Coastal Seascape

Red Rock Canyon

Fruit Medley

The Winding Lake

Fruit Placemat

New Mexico Evening Flight

Sunflowers (from front cover and personal collection of
Vicki Julian)

The Golden Bloom (from back cover)

Malibu Coastal Seascape

Red Rock Canyon

Fruit Medley

The Winding Lake

Fruit Placemat

New Mexico Evening Flight

JOAN'S FAVORITE RECIPES

<u>Chili</u>

1 ½ lbs. ground chuck beef
½ c chopped onions
½ c chopped celery
½ t salt
½ t sugar
1 t black pepper
1/12 T William's Chili Seasoning
1 can (8 oz) tomato sauce
1 can water
1 can (15 oz) red or pinto beans

Crumble and brown beef in large skillet or 2 quart pan. Stir in onions and celery and simmer until brown. Stir in salt, pepper, and chili seasoning and add tomato sauce and beans. Simmer 10-15 minutes or longer.

Note: Chili may be topped with a shredded cheese or onions when served. (Ground pork or turkey can also be substituted for beef)

Alamo Sandwiches

Rye or pumpernickel bread
Fill with:
Bacon
Swiss cheese
Ortega green chilies (midsize can)
Pace picante sauce

Butter both sides of the sandwich and grill. Fill with bacon, cheese, and green chilies.
Cut in strips and dip in Pace chunky salsa.

Lemon Meringue Pie

1 c sugar
3 T cornstarch
1 ½ c cold water
3 egg yolks, slightly beaten
Grated rind of 1 lemon
1 ¼ c lemon juice
1 T butter
1 baked 9" pie shell

Place water in a 2-quart saucepan, and stir in 1 cup sugar and the cornstarch. Add egg yolks, stirring until mixture thickens.
Remove from heat and add butter, lemon juice and rind. Let cool and then pour into baked pie shell.

Meringue: 3 egg whites 1/3 c sugar

In small bowl, beat egg whites and sugar until stiff peaks form. Spread over pie filling and bake 15-20 minutes in

350° oven until browned. Let cool and serve.

Mocha Spice Cake

2/3 c shortening, butter or oil
1 t cinnamon
1 ½ c sugar
2 t cocoa
3 eggs
¾ c buttermilk
1 ¾ c flour, sifted
1 t vanilla
½ t baking powder
1t lemon extract
½ t baking soda
½ c black walnuts
½ t salt
¾ t nutmeg

Cream shortening with sugar, adding sugar gradually. Blend in beaten eggs, flour, baking powder, baking soda, salt, nutmeg, and cocoa, and add to cream mixture, alternating with buttermilk.

Blend in vanilla and lemon extract flavorings. Fold in walnuts and pour into well-greased, floured layer cake pan. Bake 40-45 minutes at 350º. Sprinkle additional walnuts on top. Cool and ice.

Icing:

Cream 3 c confectioner sugar
6 T butter
1 ½ T cocoa
1 t vanilla
1 ½ t coffee or cream
Drop additional black walnuts over the top of cake

Sweet Potato Pie

3-4 eggs, slightly beaten
3-4 sweet potatoes, cooked and mashed
1 ¼ c sugar
1 t salt
3 t ground cinnamon
3 t nutmeg
½ t ground cloves
½ c milk or Half & Half
1 T butter
10" pie crust, purchased or made

Combine all ingredients and pour into pie shell.
Bake at 350° for 50-60 minutes (until knife inserted near center comes out clean).

Cool before cutting. Garnish with whipped topping (i.e. Cool Whip) or whipped cream.

Note from the Co-Author

I met Joan Martin nearly a decade ago through a singles group at church, and we quickly became friends. The more I learned about Joan's life, I knew she needed to tell her story, and not just because she was an African-American woman who lived through some turbulent times in recent history. Her story is important because of who she is as a person, and the incredible experiences she has had.

Joan's attitude, fortitude and very nature are something to celebrate as a shining example of a life well lived. We could all take lessons from this wonderful woman who embodies a love for life and will make the most of it until her dance card on Earth is complete.

ABOUT THE CO-AUTHOR

Vicki L. Julian is an award winning author, and editor. She has written 7 prior books, and has stories in 9 anthologies including *Chicken Soup for the Soul.*

Vicki spends her time as a Stephen Minister at her church; writing books and a faith-based blog; editing; and enjoying the company of her two sons and daughters-in-law, the most wonderful grandson, and two adorable grand-dogs.

Visit www.vickijulian.com for more information.

Made in the USA
Monee, IL
28 December 2019